be like the animals

written by carol deaver

illustrated by craig thompson

the monkey is full of laughter and fun, may we have a big smile for everyone.

the rabbit is furry

and cuddly indeed,

may we be such a comfort

to someone in need.

the elephant remembers

all it has heard,

may we also remember

all of God's words.

a dog has loyalty

that never ends,

may we also be loyal

and true to our friends.

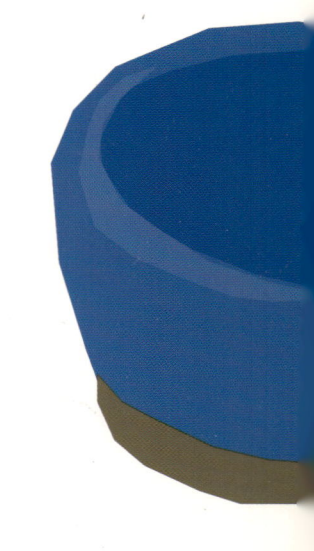

we know the giraffe is gentle and kind, as we speak to others may we keep this in mind.

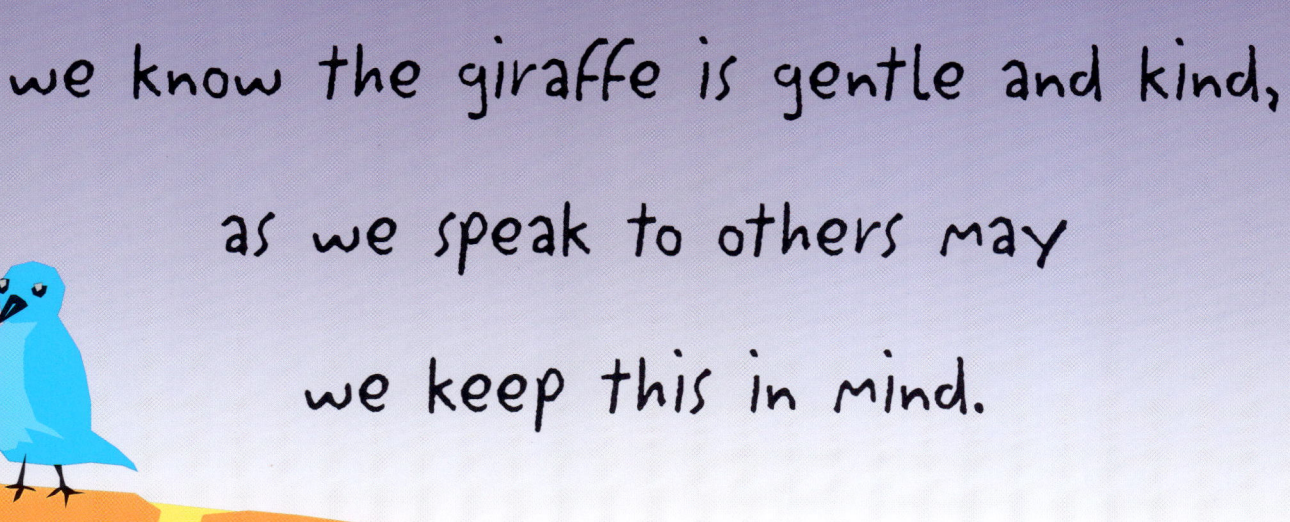

the lion is known for

courage and might,

may we have the

same courage

to do what is right.

the polar bear's coat

is white to be sure,

may it be a reminder

to us to be pure.